# Using the HTML5 Filesystem API

# Using the HTML5 Filesystem API

*Eric Bidelman*

Beijing · Cambridge · Farnham · Köln · Sebastopol · Tokyo

**Using the HTML5 Filesystem API**
by Eric Bidelman

Published by O'Reilly Media, Inc., 1005 Gravenstein Highway North, Sebastopol, CA 95472.

O'Reilly books may be purchased for educational, business, or sales promotional use. Online editions are also available for most titles (*http://my.safaribooksonline.com*). For more information, contact our corporate/institutional sales department: (800) 998-9938 or *corporate@oreilly.com*.

| | | |
|---|---|---|
| **Editors:** Mike Loukides and Meghan Blanchette | **Cover Designer:** Karen Montgomery | |
| **Proofreader:** O'Reilly Production Services | **Interior Designer:** David Futato | |
| | **Illustrator:** Robert Romano | |

**Printing History:**

| | |
|---|---|
| July 2011: | First Edition. |

ISBN: 978-1-449-30945-9

[LSI]

1311183204

# Table of Contents

# Preface

## Conventions Used in This Book

The following typographical conventions are used in this book:

*Italic*
> Indicates new terms, URLs, email addresses, filenames, and file extensions.

Constant width
> Used for program listings, as well as within paragraphs to refer to program elements such as variable or function names, databases, data types, environment variables, statements, and keywords.

**Constant width bold**
> Shows commands or other text that should be typed literally by the user.

*Constant width italic*
> Shows text that should be replaced with user-supplied values or by values determined by context.

> This icon signifies a tip, suggestion, or general note.

> This icon indicates a warning or caution.

## Using Code Examples

This book is here to help you get your job done. In general, you may use the code in this book in your programs and documentation. You do not need to contact us for permission unless you're reproducing a significant portion of the code. For example, writing a program that uses several chunks of code from this book does not require permission. Selling or distributing a CD-ROM of examples from O'Reilly books does require permission. Answering a question by citing this book and quoting example code does not require permission. Incorporating a significant amount of example code from this book into your product's documentation does require permission.

We appreciate, but do not require, attribution. An attribution usually includes the title, author, publisher, and ISBN. For example: "*Using the HTML5 Filesystem API* by Eric Bidelman (O'Reilly). Copyright 2011 Eric Bidelman, 978-1-449-30945-9."

If you feel your use of code examples falls outside fair use or the permission given above, feel free to contact us at *permissions@oreilly.com*.

## Safari® Books Online

**Safari** Safari Books Online is an on-demand digital library that lets you easily search over 7,500 technology and creative reference books and videos to find the answers you need quickly.

With a subscription, you can read any page and watch any video from our library online. Read books on your cell phone and mobile devices. Access new titles before they are available for print, and get exclusive access to manuscripts in development and post feedback for the authors. Copy and paste code samples, organize your favorites, download chapters, bookmark key sections, create notes, print out pages, and benefit from tons of other time-saving features.

O'Reilly Media has uploaded this book to the Safari Books Online service. To have full digital access to this book and others on similar topics from O'Reilly and other publishers, sign up for free at *http://my.safaribooksonline.com*.

## How to Contact Us

Please address comments and questions concerning this book to the publisher:

> O'Reilly Media, Inc.
> 1005 Gravenstein Highway North
> Sebastopol, CA 95472
> 800-998-9938 (in the United States or Canada)
> 707-829-0515 (international or local)
> 707-829-0104 (fax)

We have a web page for this book, where we list errata, examples, and any additional information. You can access this page at:

> *http://www.oreilly.com/catalog/9781449309459*

To comment or ask technical questions about this book, send email to:

> *bookquestions@oreilly.com*

For more information about our books, courses, conferences, and news, see our website at *http://www.oreilly.com*.

Find us on Facebook: *http://facebook.com/oreilly*

Follow us on Twitter: *http://twitter.com/oreillymedia*

Watch us on YouTube: *http://www.youtube.com/oreillymedia*

# CHAPTER 1

# Introduction

As we move from an offline world to a completely online world, we're demanding more from the Web, and more from web applications. Browser implementers are adding richer APIs by the day to support complex use cases. APIs for things like real-time communication, graphics, and client-side (offline) storage.

One area where the Web has lacked for some time is file I/O. Interacting with binary data and organizing that data into a meaningful hierarchy of folders is something desktop software has been capable of for decades. How amazing would it be if web apps could do the same? The lack of true filesystem access has hindered web applications from moving forward. For example, how can a photo gallery work offline without being able to save images locally? The answer is it can't! We need something more powerful.

The HTML5 File API: Directories and System (*http://dev.w3.org/2009/dap/file-system/ file-dir-sys.html*) aims to fill this void. The specification defines a means for web applications to read, create, navigate, and write to a sandboxed section of the user's local filesystem. The entirety of the Filesystem API can be broken down into a number of different related specifications:

- Reading and manipulating files: `File/Blob`, `FileList`, `FileReader`
- Creating and writing: `BlobBuilder`, `FileWriter`
- Directories and filesystem access: `DirectoryReader`, `FileEntry/DirectoryEntry`, `LocalFileSystem`

The specification defines two versions (asynchronous and synchronous) of the same API. The asynchronous API is useful for normal applications and prevents blocking UI actions. The synchronous API is reserved for use in Web Workers.

## Use Cases

HTML5 has several storage options available. The Filesystem API is different in that it aims to satisfy client-side storage use cases not well served by databases such as IndexedDB or WebSQL DB. Generally, these are applications that deal with large binary blobs and share data with applications outside of the context of the browser. The specification lists several use cases worth highlighting:

- Persistent uploader
  - When a file or directory is selected for upload, it copies the files into a local sandbox and uploads a chunk at a time.
  - Uploads can be restarted after browser crashes, network interruptions, etc.
- Video game, music, or other apps with lots of media assets
  - It downloads one or several large tarballs, and expands them locally into a directory structure.
  - The same download works on any operating system.
  - It can manage prefetching just the next-to-be-needed assets in the background, so going to the next game level or activating a new feature doesn't require waiting for a download.
  - It uses those assets directly from its local cache, by direct file reads or by handing local URIs to image or video tags, WebGL asset loaders, etc.
  - The files may be of arbitrary binary format.
  - On the server side, a compressed tarball is often much smaller than a collection of separately compressed files. Also, one tarball instead of a 1,000 little files involves fewer seeks.
- Audio/Photo editor with offline access or local cache for speed
  - The data blobs are potentially quite large, and are read-write.
  - It might want to do partial writes to files (overwriting just the ID3/EXIF tags, for example).
  - The ability to organize project files by creating directories is important.
  - Edited files should be accessible by client-side applications (iTunes, Picasa).
- Offline video viewer
  - It downloads large files (>1 GB) for later viewing.
  - It needs efficient seek and streaming.
  - It should be able to hand a URI to the video tag.
  - It should enable access to partly downloaded files (for example, to let you watch the first episode of the DVD even if your download didn't complete before you got on the plane.)
  - It should be able to pull a single episode out of the middle of a download and give just that to the video tag.
- Offline web mail client
  - Downloads attachments and stores them locally.
  - Caches user-selected attachments for later upload.

—Needs to be able to refer to cached attachments and image thumbnails for display and upload.

—Should be able to trigger the UA's download manager just as if talking to a server.

—Should be able to upload an email with attachments as a multipart post, rather than sending a file at a time in an XHR.

## Security Considerations

The HTML5 Filesystem API can be used to read and write data to parts of the user's hard drive. Because of this privileged access, there are a number of security and privacy issues that have been considered in the API's design. A few are listed below:

* Local disk usage and IO bandwidth—this is mitigated in part through quota limitations. See Chapter 2, *Storage and Quota*.

* Leakage or erasure of private data—this is mitigated by limiting the scope of the HTML5 filesystem to a chroot-like, origin-specific sandbox. Applications cannot access another domain/origin's filesystem.

* Storing malicious executables or illegal data on a user's system—with any download there is a risk. The API mitigates against malicious executables by restricting file creation/rename to nonexecutable extensions, and by making sure the execute bit is not set on any file created or modified via the API.

## Browser Support

At the time of writing, Google Chrome is the only browser to implement the Filesystem API. Version 8 of the browser was the first to see a partial implementation, but the majority of the API was later completed in version 11. In Chrome 13, a Chapter 2, *Storage and Quota* API was added to give applications a way to request addition space for storing data.

## A Cautionary Tale

Before we dive in, I want to remind you that this book covers a working implementation of an evolving specification, a spec that has yet to be finalized by the World Wide Web Consortium (W3C). Take my word of caution and realize that until the spec is final, portions of the API could change.

# CHAPTER 2

# Storage and Quota

The HTML5 Filesystem API gives applications the facility to write and store actual files in JavaScript. That is amazing, but with great power comes great responsibility. Websites now have the potential to store large amounts of binary data on a user's system. It is important that applications do not abuse such a gift by, for example, eating up large amounts of disk space without the user's knowledge or consent. The last thing users want is to have 20 GB of data stored on their system just by visiting a URL.

At the time of writing, Chrome has a limited UI settings page for users to manage the storage space for applications that save data on their behalf. It is accessible via Preferences→Under the Hood→All Cookies and Site Data (or by opening *chrome://settings/cookies*). Users can only delete data from this menu. As a result of this limited UI, write operations (such as creating a folder and writing to a file) require an application to ask for the estimated size, in bytes, they expect to use. The same practice is true for other offline storage APIs, like WebSQL DB, where one opens a database with a particular size:

```
var db = window.openDatabase(
  'MyDB',          // dbName
  '1.0',           // version
  'test database', // description
  2 * 1024 * 1024, // estimatedSize in bytes (2MB)
  function(db) {}  // optional creationCallback
);
```

## Storage Types

A normal web application can request storage space under two classifications: temporary or persistent. In addition to these types, Chrome Extensions and hosted web applications listed in the Chrome Web Store have a third option: unlimited storage.

## Temporary Storage

Temporary storage is easiest to obtain. In fact, you don't even need to request it. By default, origins are given a modest amount of temporary storage, meaning they can use temporary storage without special permissions or the browser prompting the user to take some action. Temporary storage is perfect for things like caching.

In Google Chrome 13, the HTML5 Filesystem and the WebSQL DB share a pool of disk space that sites can collectively consume. A single site can consume up to 20% of the pool. As usage of the temporary pool approaches the limit for the pool as a whole (1 GB), least recently used data will be reclaimed. Eventually, Application Cache and IndexedDB will also share in this temporary pool. Such a unified quota system also means there is no longer a 5 MB limit imposed on WebSQL DB.

 When the browser deletes temporary data it deletes all the data stored for the origin. This guarantees data won't be corrupt in an unexpected way.

Properties of temporary storage:

- Browser does not prompt the user on first use.
- Apps are granted a reasonable amount of temporary storage by default.
- Data is not guaranteed to still exist. It might be deleted at the browser's discretion when the local disk's available space.

## Persistent Storage

Persistent storage is just that, persistent. Data saved using this option is available on subsequent accesses to the same filesystem. Keep in mind, though, that even persistent data can be deleted manually by the user (either through a browser settings page or through direct filesystem operations on the OS). So the data you save is never 100% guaranteed to be there.

A key difference from temporary storage is that the browser asks the user for permission before allocating persistent storage space. In Chrome, this displays as an info bar (see Figure 2-1).

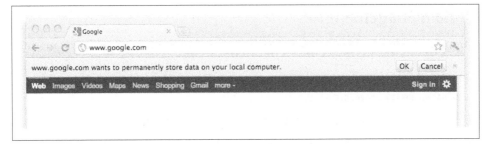

*Figure 2-1. The browser prompts the user when persistent storage is requested*

Because user intervention is involved in this storage option, apps are granted zero persistent quota by default. Any attempts to store more data than the granted quota will fail with `QUOTA_EXCEEDED_ERR`.

Properties of `PERSISTENT` storage:

- Browser prompts the user if additional space is requested.
- Apps are granted zero quota by default.
- If more storage space is needed, it can be requested. There is no fixed size storage pool.
- Data is guaranteed to be available on subsequent accesses.

## Unlimited Storage

Unlimited storage is a unique option to Chrome Extensions and Apps listed in the Chrome Web Store (either hosted or installed). Using the `unlimitedStorage` permission in the .manifest file (*http://code.google.com/chrome/extensions/manifest.html*), one can bypass the restricts of temporary and persistent storage. Think of unlimited storage as persistent storage, but without a user prompt and maximum cap.

Properties of `unlimitedStorage`:

- Exclusive to Chrome Apps and Extensions.
- Unlimited quota is granted with no user prompts (except at installation time).
- No need to request more storage when more is needed.

 Chrome can be run with an `--unlimited-quota-for-files` flag, which also allows unlimited storage. However, flags are temporary and should only be used for testing purposes. Running your primary browser with this flag gives free reign to an application, allowing it to store as much data on your hard drive as it wants. You should only use `--unlimited-quota-for-files` during testing.

# Quota Management API

Chrome 13 added a quota management API to give applications a tool for requesting, managing, and most importantly, querying the current amount of storage their origin is taking up. The API is exposed as a new global object, `webkitStorageInfo`:

```
window.webkitStorageInfo
```

The quota API is prefixed because it is not standardized yet. It has two methods:

`queryUsageAndQuota (type, opt_successCallback, opt_errorCallback);`

type
: The type of storage to return the current usage for. Possible values are TEMPO RARY or PERSISTENT.

opt_successCallback
: An optional two parameter callback. The parameters are the current number of bytes the app is using and current quota, also in bytes.

opt_errorCallback
: An optional error callback.

`requestQuota (type, size, opt_successCallback, opt_errorCallback);`

type
: Whether the new/additional storage should be persistent or temporary. Possible values are TEMPORARY or PERSISTENT.

opt_successCallback
: An optional callback passed the granted quota in bytes.

opt_errorCallback
: An optional error callback.

## Requesting More Storage

To request new or additional storage space, call `requestQuota()` with the type of storage, size, and a success callback. As explained in the previous section, the browser prompts the user with a permission bar when PERSISTENT storage is requested. If the size passed to `requestQuota()` is less than the app's current allocation, no prompt is shown. The current quota is kept. If your app is requesting additional space (e.g., the new size is larger than the app's existing quota), the user will be reprompted to accept that change. If the request is for TEMPORARY storage, again, no prompt will appear but other data may be evicted at the browsers discretion.

The following example requests 2 MB of PERSISTENT storage:

```
window.webkitStorageInfo.requestQuota(PERSISTENT, 2*1024*1024, function(bytes) {
  console.log('Granted ' + bytes + ' bytes in persistent storage');
}, function(e) {
  console.log('Error', e);
});
```

## Checking Current Usage

To query the current storage usage and quota of an application, call `queryUsageAnd Quota()` with the type of storage you're interested in checking and a success callback. This method returns two things to your callback, the number of bytes being used, and the total quota for the storage type in question.

For example, if example.com wanted to check the percentage of TEMPORARY storage it is using, it could run:

```
window.webkitStorageInfo.queryUsageAndQuota(TEMPORARY, function(usage, quota) {
    console.log('Using: ' + (usage / quota) * 100 + '% of temporary storage');
}, function(e) {
    console.log('Error', e);
});
```

The usage reported by the quota API might not precisely match the size that was requested using `requestQuota()` or the actual size of the stored data on disk. The discrepancy comes from each storage type needing some extra bytes to store meta data. There may also be some time lag until updates are reflected to the quota API.

# CHAPTER 3

# Getting Started

## Opening a Filesystem

A web application obtains access to the HTML5 Filesystem by requesting a `LocalFile System` object using a global method, `window.requestFileSystem()`:

```
window.requestFileSystem(type, size, successCallback, opt_errorCallback)
```

 This method is currently vendor prefixed as `window.webkitRequestFile System`.

Its parameters are described below:

`type`
Whether the storage should be persistent. Possible values are `TEMPORARY` or `PERSIS TENT`. Data stored using `TEMPORARY` can be removed at the browser's discretion (for example if more space is needed). `PERSISTENT` storage cannot cleared unless explicitly authorized by the user or the application.

`size`
An indicator of how much storage space, in bytes, the application expects to need.

`successCallback`
A callback function that is called when the user agent successfully provides a filesystem. Its argument is a `FileSystem` object.

`opt_errorCallback`
An optional callback function which is called when an error occurs, or the request for a filesystem is denied. Its argument is a `FileError` object.

Calling `window.requestFileSystem()` for the first time creates a new sandboxed storage space for the app and origin that requested it. A filesystem is restricted to a single application and cannot access another application's stored data. This also means that an application cannot read/write files to an arbitrary folder on the user's hard drive (such as My Pictures or My Documents). Each filesystem is isolated.

*Example 3-1. Requesting a filesystem temporary storage*

```
var onError = function(fs) {
  console.log('There was an error');
};

var onFS = function(fs) {
  console.log('Opened filesystem: ' + fs.name);
};

window.requestFileSystem(window.TEMPORARY, 5*1024*1024 /*5MB*/, onFs, onError);
```

If all goes well, the success callback (`onFS`) is called and passed a `FileSystem` object containing two properties:

name
> A unique name for the filesystem, assigned by the browser

root
> A read-only `DirectoryEntry` representing the root of the filesystem

The `FileSystem` object is your gateway to the entire API. Once you have a reference, it's worth caching it in a global variable or class property. You'll use it all over the place.

Things get a bit more complicated when using persistent storage with the filesystem. The previous chapter explained that applications are granted zero persistent quota by default. As a result, you need to request some persistent quota before opening the filesystem. That might mean simply wrapping the call to `window.requestFileSystem()` in the `requestQuota()` callback.

*Example 3-2. Requesting a filesystem with persistent storage*

```
const SIZE = 5*1024*1024; /*5MB*/
const TYPE = PERSISTENT;

window.webkitStorageInfo.requestQuota(TYPE, SIZE, function(grantedBytes) {
  window.requestFileSystem(TYPE, grantedBytes, onFs, onError);
}, function(e) {
  console.log('Error', e);
});
```

After the user grants permission to use persistent storage, your app is allocated the amount of quota it requested. There's no need to ask for more quota until space becomes an issue. When that point comes, the best way to recover is to attempt the write operation, catch the `QUOTA_EXCEEDED_ERR` in the error callback, and request more persistent storage using `requestQuota()`. Don't worry if none of that makes sense now. It will in the next chapter, Chapter 4, *Working with Files*.

# Handling Errors

Error callbacks are optional arguments to the API's methods. However, it is always a good idea to catch errors for users, as there are a number of places where things can go wrong. For example, if you run out of quota, write access to the filesystem is denied, or a disk I/O operation fails.

Error callbacks are passed `FileError` objects, which contain a code corresponding to the type of error that occurred. The code can be compared to the enum constants in `FileError`.

*Example 3-3. Generic error handler*

```
function onError(err) {
  var msg = 'Error: ';

  switch (err.code) {
    case FileError.NOT_FOUND_ERR:
      msg += 'File or directory not found';
      break;
    case FileError.SECURITY_ERR:
      msg += 'Insecure or disallowed operation';
      break;
    case FileError.ABORT_ERR:
      msg += 'Operation aborted';
      break;
    case FileError.NOT_READABLE_ERR:
      msg += 'File or directory not readable';
      break;
    case FileError.ENCODING_ERR:
      msg += 'Invalid encoding';
      break;
    case FileError.NO_MODIFICATION_ALLOWED_ERR:
      msg += 'Cannot modify file or directory';
      break;
    case FileError.INVALID_STATE_ERR:
      msg += 'Invalid state';
      break;
    case FileError.SYNTAX_ERR:
      msg += 'Invalid line-ending specifier';
      break;
    case FileError.INVALID_MODIFICATION_ERR:
      msg += 'Invalid modification';
      break;
    case FileError.QUOTA_EXCEEDED_ERR:
      msg += 'Storage quota exceeded';
      break;
    case FileError.TYPE_MISMATCH_ERR:
      msg += 'Invalid filetype';
      break;
    case FileError.PATH_EXISTS_ERR:
      msg += 'File or directory already exists at specified path';
      break;
    default:
```

```
      msg += 'Unknown Error';
      break;
  };

  console.log(msg);
}
```

 Instead of comparing directly to the `FileError` constants, you may want
to extend its prototype with a `name` attribute that translates error codes
to their mnemonic key:

```
FileError.prototype.__defineGetter__('name', function() {
  var keys = Object.keys(FileError);
  for (var i = 0, key; key = keys[i]; ++i) {
    if (FileError[key] == this.code) {
      return key;
    }
  }
  return 'Unknown Error';
});

function onError(err) {
  console.log(err.name);
  // e.g., 'QUOTA_EXCEEDED_ERR', 'NOT_READABLE_ERR', etc.
}
```

# CHAPTER 4

# Working with Files

## The FileEntry

Files in the sandboxed filesystem are represented by the `FileEntry` interface. A `FileEntry` contains the types of properties and methods one would expect from a standard filesystem.

**Properties**

`isFile`
> Boolean. True if the entry is a file.

`isDirectory`
> Boolean. True if the entry is a directory.

`name`
> DOMString. The name of the entry, excluding the path leading to it.

`fullPath`
> DOMString. The full absolute path from the root to the entry.

`filesystem`
> FileSystem. The filesystem on which the entry resides.

**Methods**

`getMetadata (successCallback, opt_errorCallback)`
> Look up metadata about this entry.

`moveTo (parentDirEntry, opt_newName, opt_successCallback, opt_errorCallback)`
> Move an entry to a different location on the filesystem.

`copyTo (parentDirEntry, opt_newName, opt_successCallback, opt_errorCallback)`
> Copies an entry to a different parent on the filesystem. Directory copies are always recursive. It is an error to copy a directory inside itself or to copy it into its parent if a new name is not provided.

`toURL ();`
> Returns a `filesystem:` URL that can be used to identify this file. See Chapter 7.

remove (successCallback, opt_errorCallback)
> Deletes a file or directory. It is an error to attempt to delete the root directory of a filesystem or a directory that is not empty.

getParent (successCallback, opt_errorCallback)
> Return the parent `DirectoryEntry` containing this entry. If this entry is the root directory, its parent is itself.

createWriter (successCallback, opt_errorCallback)
> Creates a new `FileWriter` (See "Writing to a File" on page 18) which can be used to write content to this `FileEntry`.

file (successCallback, opt_errorCallback)
> Returns a `File` representing the `FileEntry` to the success callback.

To better understand `FileEntry`, the rest of this chapter contains code recipes for performing common tasks.

# Creating a File

After "Opening a Filesystem" on page 11, the `FileSystem` that is passed to the success callback contains the root `DirectoryEntry` (as `fs.root`). To look up or create a file in this directory, call its `getFile()`, passing the name of the file to create.

For example, the following code creates an empty file called *log.txt* in the root directory.

*Example 4-1. Creating a file and printing its last modified time*

```
function onFs(fs) {

  fs.root.getFile('log.txt', {create: true, exclusive: true},
      function(fileEntry) {
        // fileEntry.isFile === true
        // fileEntry.name == 'log.txt'
        // fileEntry.fullPath == '/log.txt'

        fileEntry.getMetaData(function(md) {
          console.log(md.modificationTime.toDateString());
        }, onError);

      },
      onError
  );
}

window.requestFileSystem(TEMPORARY, 1024*1024 /*1MB*/, onFs, onError);
```

The first argument to getFile() can be an absolute or relative path, but it must be valid. For instance, it is an error to attempt to create a file whose immediate parent does not exist. The second argument is an object literal describing the function's behavior if the file does not exist. In this example, create: true creates the file if it doesn't exist and throws an error if it does (exclusive: true). Otherwise if create: false, the file is simply fetched and returned. By itself, the exclusive option has no effect. In either case, the file contents are not overwritten. We're simply obtaining a reference entry to the file in question.

## Reading a File by Name

Calling getFile() only retrieves a FileEntry. It does not return the contents of a file. For that, we need a File object and the FileReader API. To obtain a File, call FileEntry.file(). Its first argument is a success callback which is passed the file, and its second is an error callback.

The following code retrieves the file named *log.txt*. Its contents are read into memory as text using the FileReader API, and the result is appended to the DOM as a new <textarea>. If *log.txt* does not exist, an error is thrown.

*Example 4-2. Reading a text file*

```
function onFs(fs) {

  fs.root.getFile('log.txt', {}, function(fileEntry) {

    // Obtain the File object representing the FileEntry.
    // Use FileReader to read its contents.
    fileEntry.file(function(file) {
      var reader = new FileReader();

      reader.onloadend = function(e) {
        var textarea = document.createElement('textarea');
        textarea = this.result;
        document.body.appendChild(textarea);
      };

      reader.readAsText(file); // Read the file as plaintext.
    }, onError);

  }, onError);

}

window.requestFileSystem(TEMPORARY, 1024*1024 /*1MB*/, onFs, onError);
```

# Writing to a File

The API exposes the `FileWriter` (*http://dev.w3.org/2009/dap/file-system/file-writer.html*) interface for writing content to a `FileEntry`.

## Properties

`position`
> Integer. The byte offset at which the next write will occur. For example, a newly-created `FileWriter` has position set to 0.

`length`
> Integer. The length of the file.

`error`
> `FileError`. The last error that occurred.

`readyState`
> One of 3 states: `INIT`, `WRITING`, `DONE`.

## Methods

`abort ()`
> Aborts a write operation in progress. If `readyState` is `DONE` or `INIT`, an `INVALID_STATE_ERR` exception is thrown.

`write (blob)`
> Writes the supplied data to the file, starting at the offset given by `position`. The argument can be a `Blob` or `File` object.

`seek (offset)`
> Sets the file `position` at which the next write occurs. The argument is a byte offset into the file. If offset > length, length is used instead. If offset is < 0, `position` is set back from the end of the file.

`truncate (size)`
> Changes the `length` of the file to a new size. Shortening the file discards any data beyond the new length. Extending it beyond the current length zero-pads the existing data up to the new `length`.

## Events

`onabort`
> Called when an in-progress write operation is cancelled.

`onerror`
> Called when an error occurs.

`onprogress`
> Called periodically as data is being written.

`onwrite`
> Called when the write operation has successfully completed.

onwritestart
> Called just before writing is about to start.

onwriteend
> Called when the write is complete, whether successful or not.

The following code creates an empty file called *log.txt* in a subfolder, */temp*. If the file already exists, it is simple retrieved. The text "Lorem Ipsum" is written to it by constructing a new `Blob` using the BlobBuilder (*http://dev.w3.org/2009/dap/file-system/file -writer.html#idl-def-BlobBuilder*) API, and handing it off to `FileWriter.write()`. Event handlers are set up to monitor `error` and `writeend` events.

*Example 4-3. Writing text to a file*

```
function onFs(fs) {

  fs.root.getFile('/temp/log.txt', {create: true}, function(fileEntry) {

    // Create a FileWriter object for our FileEntry.
    fileEntry.createWriter(function(fileWriter) {

      fileWriter.onwrite = function(e) {
        console.log('Write completed.');
      };

      fileWriter.onerror = function(e) {
        console.log('Write failed: ' + e.toString());
      };

      var bb = new BlobBuilder(); // Create a new Blob on-the-fly.
      bb.append('Lorem Ipsum');

      fileWriter.write(bb.getBlob('text/plain'));

    }, onError);

  }, onError);

}

window.requestFileSystem(TEMPORARY, 1024*1024 /*1MB*/, onFs, onError);
```

> The BlobBuilder API has been vendor prefixed in Firefox 6 and Chrome:
>
> ```
> window.BlobBuilder = window.BlobBuilder || window.WebKitBlob
> Builder || window.MozBlobBuilder;
> ```

If the folder */temp* did not exist in the filesystem, an error is thrown.

## Appending Data to a File

Appending data onto an existing file is trivial with `FileWriter`. We can reposition the writer to the end of the file using `seek()`. Seek takes a byte offset as an argument, setting the file writer's `position` to that offset. If the offset is greater than the file's length, the current length is used instead. If offset is < 0, `position` is set back from the end of the file.

As an example, the following snippet appends a timestamp to the end of a log file. An error is thrown if the file does not yet exist.

*Example 4-4. Logging a timestamp*

```
window.BlobBuilder = window.BlobBuilder || window.WebKitBlobBuilder ||
                     window.MozBlobBuilder;

function append(fs, filePath, blob) {
  fs.root.getFile(filePath, {create: false}, function(fileEntry) {

    // Create a FileWriter object for our FileEntry.
    fileEntry.createWriter(function(fileWriter) {

      fileWriter.seek(fileWriter.length); // Start write position at EOF.
      fileWriter.write(bb.getBlob('text/plain'));

    }, onError);

  }, onError);
}

function onFs(fs) {
  var bb = new BlobBuilder();
  bb.append((new Date()).toISOString() + '\n');

  append(fs, 'log.txt', bb.getBlob('text/plain'));
}

window.requestFileSystem(TEMPORARY, 1024*1024 /*1MB*/, onFs, onError);
```

# Importing Files

For security reasons, the HTML5 Filesystem API does not allow applications to write data outside of their sandbox. As a result of this restriction, applications cannot share filesystems and they cannot read or write files to arbitrary folders on the user's hard drive, such as their My Pictures or My Music folder. This leaves developers in a bit of a predicament. How does one import files into a web application if the application cannot access the user's full hard drive with all of their precious files?

There are four techniques to import data into the filesystem:

- Use `<input type="file">`. The user selects files from a location on their machine and the application duplicates those files into the app's HTML5 filesystem.

- Use HTML5 drag and drop. Some browsers support dragging in files from the desktop to the browser tab. Again, the selected files would be duplicated into the HTML5 filesystem.

- Use XMLHttpRequest. New properties in XMLHttpRequest 2 (*http://dev.w3.org/2006/webapi/XMLHttpRequest-2/*) make it trivial to fetch remote binary data, then store that data locally using the HTML5 filesystem.

- Using copy and paste events. Apps can read clipboard information that contains file data.

## Using <input type="file">

The first (and most common) way to import files into an app is to repurpose our old friend <input type="file">. I say repurpose because we're not interested in uploading form data—the typical usage of a file input. Instead, we can utilize the browser's native file picker, prompt users to select files, and save those selections into our app.

The following example allows users to select multiple files using <input type="file" multiple> and creates copies of those files in the app's sandboxed filesystem.

*Example 4-5. Duplicating user-selected files*

```
<input type="file" id="myfile" multiple />

// Creates a file if it doesn't exist.
// Throws an error if a file already exists with the same name.

var writeFile = function(parentDirectory, file) {
  parentDirectory.getFile(file.name, {create: true, exclusive: true},
      function(fileEntry) {

        fileEntry.createWriter(function(fileWriter) {
          fileWriter.write(file);
        }, onError);

      },
      onError
  );
};

document.querySelector("input[type='file']").onchange = function(e) {
  var files = this.files;

  window.requestFileSystem(TEMPORARY, 1024*1024 /*1MB*/, function(fs) {
    for (var i = 0, file; file = files[i]; ++i){
      writeFile(fs.root, file);
    }
  }, onError);
};
```

As noted in the comment, `FileWriter.write()` accepts a `Blob` or `File`. This is because `File` inherits from `Blob`, and therefore, all files are blobs. The reverse is not true.

Consider allowing users to import an entire folder using `<input type="file" webkidir ectory>`. By including this attribute, the browser allows users to select a folder and recursively read all the files in it. The result is a `FileList` of every file in the folder.

*Example 4-6. Importing a directory*

```
<input type="file" id="myfile" webkitdirectory />

// Creates a file if it doesn't exist.
// Throw an error if a file already exists with the same name.

var writeFile = function(parentDirectory, file) {
  parentDirectory.getFile(file.name, {create: true, exclusive: true},
      function(fileEntry) {

        // Write the file. write() can take a File or Blob.
        fileEntry.createWriter(function(fileWriter) {
          fileWriter.write(file);
        }, onError);

      },
      onError
  );
};

document.querySelector("#myfile").onchange = function(e) {
  for (var i = 0, f; f = e.target.files[i]; ++i) {
    console.log(f.webkitRelativePath);
  }
};
```

What's not shown in the above example is the writing of each file to the proper direc-tory. Creating folders is covered in the next chapter.

## Using HTML5 Drag and Drop

The second method for importing files is to use HTML5 drag and drop (*http://dev.w3 .org/html5/spec-author-view/dnd.html*). Some people love it. Some people hate it. But whether or not you're a fan of HTML5's drag and drop design, it is here to stay. That said, one really nice thing drag and drop gives us is a familiar way for users to import data into our web applications.

Chrome, Safari 5, and Firefox 4 extend HTML5 drag and drop events by allowing files to be dragged in from the desktop to the browser window. In fact, the process for setting up event listeners to handle dropped file(s) is exactly the same as handling other types of content. The only difference is the way the files are accessed in the drop handler. Typically, dropped data is read from the event's `dataTransfer` property (as `dataTrans fer.getData()`). However, when handling files, data is read from `dataTransfer.files`.

If that looks suspiciously familiar, it should be! This is the drag and drop equivalent of the previous example using `<input type="file">`.

The following example allows users to drag in files from the desktop. On the **dragenter** and **dragleave** events, the class "dropping" is toggled to give the user a visual indication a drop can occur.

*Example 4-7. Importing files using drag and drop from the desktop*

```
<!DOCTYPE html>
<html>
<head>
<meta charset="utf-8">
<title>Drag and drop files</title>
<style>
.dropping {
  background: -webkit-repeating-radial-gradient(white, #fc0 5px);
  background: -moz-repeating-radial-gradient(white, #fc0 5px);
  background: -ms-repeating-radial-gradient(white, #fc0 5px);
  background: -o-repeating-radial-gradient(white, #fc0 5px);
  background: repeating-radial-gradient(white, #fc0 5px);
}
</style>
</head>
<body>

<p>Drag files in from your desktop. They will be added to the filesystem.</p>

<script>
window.requestFileSystem = window.requestFileSystem ||
                           window.webkiRequestFileSystem;

/**
 * Class to handle drag and drop events on an element.
 *
 * @param {string} selector A CSS selector for an element to attach drag and
 *     drop events to.
 * @param {function(FileList)} onDropCallback A callback passed the list of
 *     files that were dropped.
 * @constructor
 */
function DnDFileController(selector, onDropCallback) {
  var el_ = document.querySelector(selector);

  this.dragenter = function(e) {
    e.stopPropagation();
    e.preventDefault();

    // Give a visual indication this element is a drop target.
    el_.classList.add('dropping');
  };

  this.dragover = function(e) {
    e.stopPropagation();
    e.preventDefault();
```

```
  };

  this.dragleave = function(e) {
    e.stopPropagation();
    e.preventDefault();
    el_.classList.remove('dropping');
  };

  this.drop = function(e) {
    e.stopPropagation();
    e.preventDefault();

    el_.classList.remove('dropping');

    onDropCallback(e.dataTransfer.files);
  };

  el_.addEventListener('dragenter', this.dragenter, false);
  el_.addEventListener('dragover', this.dragover, false);
  el_.addEventListener('dragleave', this.dragleave, false);
  el_.addEventListener('drop', this.drop, false);
};

var FS = null; // Cache the FileSystem object for later use.

// Allow dropping onto the entire page.
var controller = new DnDFileController('body', function(files) {
  [].forEach.call(files, function(file, i) {
    // See Example 4-5 for the defintion of writeFile().
    writeFile(FS.root, file);
  });
});

(function openFS() {
  window.requestFileSystem(TEMPORARY, 1024*1024 /*1MB*/, function(fs) {
    FS = fs;
  }, onError);
})();
</script>
</body>
</html>
```

## Using XMLHttpRequest

A third way to import data is to use XMLHttpRequest to fetch remote files. The difference
between this method and the first two methods is that this option requires data to
already exist somewhere in the cloud. In most cases that's not a problem. As web
developers, we have learned to deal with remote data and encounter it all the time.

Many of the enhancements put into XMLHttpRequest Level 2 (*http://dev.w3.org/2006/webapi/XMLHttpRequest-2/*) are designed for better interoperability with binary data, blobs, and files. This is really good news for web developers. It means we can put an end to crazy string manipulation and error-prone character code hacks in our applications. As an example of what I mean, here is one well-known trick to fetch an image as a binary string.

*Example 4-8. Old way to fetch a binary file*

```
var xhr = new XMLHttpRequest();
xhr.open('GET', '/path/to/image.png', true);

// Hack to pass bytes through unprocessed.
xhr.overrideMimeType('text/plain; charset=x-user-defined');

xhr.onreadystatechange = function(e) {
  if (this.readyState == 4 && this.status == 200) {
    var binStr = this.responseText;
    for (var i = 0, len = binStr.length; i < len; ++i) {
      var c = binStr.charCodeAt(i); // or String.fromCharCode()
      var byte = c & 0xff; // byte at offset i
      ...
    }
  }
};

xhr.send(null);
```

While this technique works, what you actually get back in the responseText is not a binary blob. It is a binary string representing the image file. We're tricking the server into passing the data back, unprocessed. Even though this little gem works, I'm going to call it black magic and advise against it. Any time you resort to character code hacks and string manipulation for coercing data into a desirable format, that's a problem. Instead, XMLHttpRequest now exposes responseType and response properties to inform the browser what format to return data in:

xhr.responseType
> After opening a new request but before sending it, set xhr.responseType to "text", "arraybuffer", "blob", or "document", depending on your data needs. Setting xhr.responseType='' or omitting altogether defaults the response to "text" (i.e., xhr.responseText === xhr.response).

xhr.response
> After a successful request, the xhr.response contains the requested data as a DOM String, ArrayBuffer, Blob, or Document, according to what xhr.responseType was set to.

With these new tools, we can clean up the previous example by reworking how the data is fetched. This time, the image is downloaded as an ArrayBuffer instead of a binary string, then handed over to the BlobBuilder API to create a Blob.

*Example 4-9. Fetch an image file as a blob and write it to the filesystem*

```html
<!DOCTYPE html>
<html>
<head>
  <meta charset="utf-8">
  <title>Fetch + write an image to the HTML5 filesystem</title>
</head>
<body>
<script>
// Take care of vendor prefixes.
window.BlobBuilder = window.BlobBuilder || window.WebKitBlobBuilder ||
                     window.MozBlobBuilder;
window.requestFileSystem = window.requestFileSystem ||
                           window.webkitRequestFileSystem;

var onError = function(e) {
  console.log('There was an error', e);
};

/**
 * Writes a Blob to the filesystem.
 *
 * @param {DirectoryEntry} dir The directory to write the blob into.
 * @param {Blob} blob The data to write.
 * @param {string} fileName A name for the file.
 * @param {function(ProgressEvent)} opt_callback An optional callback.
 *     Invoked when the write completes.
 */

var writeBlob = function(dir, blob, fileName, opt_callback) {
  dir.getFile(fileName, {create: true, exclusive: true}, function(fileEntry) {

    fileEntry.createWriter(function(writer) {
      if (opt_callback) {
        writer.onwrite = opt_callback;
      }
      writer.write(blob);
    }, onError);

  }, onError);
};

/**
 * Fetches a file by URL and writes it to the filesystem.
 *
 * @param {string} url The url the resource resides under.
 * @param {string} mimeType The content type of the file.
 */
var downloadImage = function(url, mimeType) {
  var xhr = new XMLHttpRequest();
  xhr.open('GET', url, true);
  xhr.responseType = 'arraybuffer';

  xhr.onload = function(e) {
    if (this.status == 200) {
```

```
    var bb = new BlobBuilder();
    bb.append(xhr.response); // Note: not xhr.responseText

    var parts = url.split('/');
    var fileName = parts[parts.length - 1];

    window.requestFileSystem(TEMPORARY, 1024*1024*5 /*5MB*/, function(fs) {
      var onWrite = function(evt) {
        console.log('Write completed.');
      };

      // Write file to the root directory.
      writeBlob(fs.root, bb.getBlob(mimeType), fileName, onWrite);
    }, onError);
    }
  };

  xhr.send(null);
};

if (window.requestFileSystem && window.BlobBuilder) {
  downloadImage('/path/to/image.png', 'image/png');
}
</script>
</body>
</html>
```

## Using Copy and Paste

A final way to import files involves pasting files in your application. This is done by setting up and onpaste handler on the document body and iterating through the event's clipboardData items. Each item has a "kind" and "type" property. Checking the "kind" property can be used to verify whether or not a pasted item is a file. If item.kind == "file", then the item is indeed a file.

The following example sets up an onpaste listener on the page, allowing users to paste in *.png*s. The images/items are then read as Blobs using getAsFile(), and written into the filesystem.

*Example 4-10. Pasting a file into an application and saving it to the filesystem*

```
<!DOCTYPE html>
<html>
<head>
  <meta charset="utf-8">
  <title>Pasting a file into an application and saving it to the filesystem</title>
</head>
<body>
<p>
  Copy an image from the Web (right-click > Copy Image), click in this window,
  and paste it in.
</p>
<script>
```

```javascript
// Take care of vendor prefixes.
window.requestFileSystem = window.requestFileSystem ||
                           window.webkiRequestFileSystem;
window.URL = window.URL || window.webkitURL;

var onError = function(e) {
  console.log('There was an error', e);
};

/**
 * Writes a Blob to the filesystem.
 *
 * @param {DirectoryEntry} dir The directory to write the blob into.
 * @param {Blob} blob The data to write.
 * @param {string} fileName A name for the file.
 * @param {function(ProgressEvent)} opt_callback An optional callback.
 *     Invoked when the write completes.
 */
var writeBlob = function(dir, blob, fileName, opt_callback) {
  dir.getFile(fileName, {create: true}, function(fileEntry) {

    fileEntry.createWriter(function(writer) {
      if (opt_callback) {
        writer.onwrite = opt_callback;
      }
      writer.write(blob);
    }, onError);

  }, onError);
};


// Setup onpaste handler to catch dropped .png files.
document.body.onpaste = function(e) {
  var items = e.clipboardData.items;
  for (var i = 0; i < items.length; ++i) {
    if (items[i].kind == 'file' && items[i].type == 'image/png') {
      var blob = items[i].getAsFile();

      writeBlob(FS.root, blob, 'MyPastedImage', function(e) {
        console.log('Write completed.');
      });
    }
  }
};

va FS; // cache the FileSystem object for later.
window.requestFileSystem(TEMPORARY, 1024*1024 /*1MB*/, function(fs) {
  FS = fs;
}, onError);
</script>
</body>
</html>
```

# Removing Files

To remove a file from the filesystem, call `entry.remove()`. The first argument to this method is a zero-parameter callback function, which is called when the file is successfully deleted. The second is an optional error callback if any errors occur.

*Example 4-11. Removing a file by name*

```
window.requestFileSystem(TEMPORARY, 1024*1024 /*1MB*/, function(fs) {
  fs.root.getFile('log.txt', {}, function(fileEntry) {

    fileEntry.remove(function() {
      console.log('File removed.');
    }, onError);

  }, onError);
}, onError);
```

# CHAPTER 5

# Working with Directories

## The DirectoryEntry

Directories in the sandboxed filesystem are represented by the `DirectoryEntry` interface. A `DirectoryEntry` contains many of the properties and methods found in `FileEntry`. Both inherit from a generic entry interface. However, it includes additional method for working with directories.

### Properties

`isFile`
> Boolean. True if the entry is a file.

`isDirectory`
> Boolean. True if the entry is a directory.

`name`
> DOMString. The name of the directory, excluding the path leading to it.

`fullPath`
> DOMString. The full absolute path from the root to the directory.

`filesystem`
> FileSystem. The filesystem on which the directory resides.

### Methods

`getMetadata (successCallback, opt_errorCallback)`
> Looks up metadata about this directory.

`moveTo (parentDirEntry, opt_newName, opt_successCallback, opt_errorCallback)`
> Moves the directory to a different location on the filesystem.

`copyTo (parentDirEntry, opt_newName, opt_successCallback, opt_errorCallback)`
> Copies the directory to a different parent on the filesystem. Directory copies are always recursive. It is an error to copy a directory inside itself or to copy it into its parent if a new name is not provided.

toURL ();
> Returns a `filesystem:` URL that can be used to identify this directory. See Chapter 7.

remove (successCallback, opt_errorCallback)
> Deletes a file or directory. It is an error to attempt to delete the root directory of a filesystem or a directory that is not empty.

getParent (successCallback, opt_errorCallback)
> Returns the parent `DirectoryEntry` containing this directory. If this directory is the root directory, its parent is itself.

createReader ()
> Creates a new `DirectoryReader` to read entries relative to this `DirectoryEntry`.

getFile (path, optionsObj, opt_successCallback, opt_errorCallback)
> Creates or looks up a `FileEntry`. The first argument is a path representing and absolute or relative path from this directory. The second argument is an object literal describing the behavior of this method if the file does not exist. If `create: true` and `exclusive: true`, and error is thrown if the file already exists at path. If `create: true` and `exclusive: false`, the file will be created. If it already exists, no error will be thrown. Lastly, if `create: false` the file is returned if it exists, and an error is thrown if it does not. When fetching a file, the `exclusive` flag is ignored. If success, a `FileEntry` in returned in the callback.

getDirectory (path, optionsObj, opt_successCallback, opt_errorCallback)
> Creates or looks up a `DirectoryEntry`. The semantics of this method are the same as getFile(), with the difference being a `DirectoryEntry` is passed to the success callback.

removeRecursively (successCallback, opt_errorCallback)
> Recursively deletes this directory and all of its contents. An error is thrown if you try to remove the root directory of a filesystem. If an error occurs while this method is in progress, some of the directory's contents might not be deleted.

To better understand `DirectoryEntry`, the rest of this chapter contains code recipes for performing common tasks.

# Creating Directories

A Filesystem API wouldn't be much of a Filesystem API if it did not support custom folder hierarchies. You can create or fetch a directory using `DirectoryEntry.getDirectory()`. Its semantics are exactly the same as `FileEntry.getFile()`, which was described in the previous chapter. The first parameter is a string representing an absolute or relative path of the directory to interact with. For example, the following code creates a directory named *MyPictures* in the root directory.

*Example 5-1. Creating a folder*

```
function onFs(fs) {

  fs.root.getDirectory('MyPictures', {create: true}, function(dirEntry) {

    // dirEntry.isFile === false
    // dirEntry.isDirectory === true
    // dirEntry.name == 'MyPictures'
    // dirEntry.fullPath == '/MyPictures'

  }, onError);

}

window.requestFileSystem(TEMPORARY, 1024*1024 /*1MB*/, onFs, onError);
```

## Subdirectories

In most cases, creating a subfolder is straightforward because its parent folder will already exists. The process becomes somewhat more involved when trying to create a full path all in one shot (think `mkdir -p /one/two/three` on UNIX). The API throws an error if you try to create a directory whose immediate parent does not exist. The solution is to create each directory sequentially; something that is rather tricky to do with an asynchronous API.

The following example creates a new hierarchy (*music/genres/jazz*) by recursively adding each path after its parent folder has been created.

*Example 5-2. Creating subfolders*

```
function createDir(parentDir, folders) {
  // Throw out './' or '/' and move on to prevent something like '/foo/.//bar'.
  if (folders[0] == '.' || folders[0] == '') {
    folders = folders.slice(1);
  }

  parentDir.getDirectory(folders[0], {create: true}, function(dirEntry) {
    // Recursively add the new subfolder (if we still have another to create).
    if (folders.length) {
      // Use the the created directory as the new parentDir. Process next path.
      createDir(dirEntry, folders.slice(1));
    }
  }, onError);
}

const PATH = 'music/genres/jazz/';

window.requestFileSystem(TEMPORARY, 1024*1024 /*1MB*/, function(fs) {
  createDir(fs.root, PATH.split('/')); // fs.root is a DirectoryEntry.
}, onError);
```

Once *music/genres/jazz* is in place, it becomes very simple to create files under it. We can now pass a full path to getDirectory() to create files or folders under the *jazz* directory:

```
const FILE_PATH = '/music/genres/jazz/song.mp3';
window.requestFileSystem(TEMPORARY, 1024*1024 /*1MB*/, function(fs) {
  fs.root.getFile(FILE_PATH, {create: true}, function(fileEntry) {
    ...
  }, onError);
}, onError);
```

Alternatively, if we had the DirectoryEntry representing the *jazz* folder, the previous example becomes:

```
window.requestFileSystem(TEMPORARY, 1024*1024 /*1MB*/, function(fs) {
  jazzFolder.getFile('song.mp3', {create: true}, function(fileEntry) {
    ...
  }, onError);
}, onError);
```

# Reading the Contents of a Directory

The API exposes a DirectoryReader (*http://dev.w3.org/2009/dap/file-system/file-dir-sys .html#the-directoryreader-interface*) interface for reading the entries in a directory.

**Methods**

readEntries (successCallback, opt_errorCallback)
Returns a list of entries in this directory. This method must be called until an empty array is returned.

To list all the files and folders in a DirectoryEntry, first create a DirectoryReader (a synchronous operation):

```
var reader = directoryEntry.createReader();
```

Next, call readEntries(). The API makes no guarantees that all of a entries are returned in a single call to readEntries(). You must continue to call readEntries() until no more results are returned. The following example demonstrates this.

*Example 5-3. Listing the entries in a directory*

```
<!DOCTYPE html>
<html>
<head>
  <meta charset="utf-8">
  <title>Listing the entries in a directory</title>
</head>
<body>

<ul id="filelist"></ul>

<script>
```

```javascript
// Take care of vendor prefixes.
window.requestFileSystem = window.requestFileSystem ||
                           window.webkiRequestFileSystem;

/**
 * Returns an Array from a NodeList or other array-like object.
 *
 * @param {NodeList} list An array-like object to transform into an array.
 * @return {Array} The list as an array.
 */
function toArray(list) {
  return Array.prototype.slice.call(list || [], 0);
}

/**
 * Renders a list of file/folder entries.
 *
 * @param {Array<FileEntry|DirectoryEntry>} entries A list of file/folders.
 */
function listResults(entries) {
  // Use a document fragment. Will cause only one reflow on append :)
  var fragment = document.createDocumentFragment();

  entries.forEach(function(entry, i) {
    var img = entry.isDirectory ? '<img src="folder-icon.gif">' :
                                  '<img src="file-icon.gif">';
    var li = document.createElement('li');
    li.innerHTML = [img, '<span>', entry.name, '</span>'].join('');
    fragment.appendChild(li);
  });

  document.querySelector('#filelist').appendChild(fragment);
}

window.requestFileSystem(TEMPORARY, 1024*1024 /*1MB*/, function(fs) {

  var dirReader = fs.root.createReader();
  var entries = [];

  // Call the reader.readEntries() until no more results are returned.
  var readEntries = function() {
    dirReader.readEntries(function(results) {
      // If no more results are returned, we're done.
      if (!results.length) {
        // Sort list by name of entry.
        entries.sort(function(a, b) {
          return a.name < b.name ? -1 :
                 b.name < a.name ? 1 : 0;
        });

        listResults(entries); // Render the list.

      } else {
        // Add in these results to the current list.
        entries = entries.concat(toArray(results));
```

```
      readEntries();
    }
  }, onError);
};

  readEntries(); // Start reading the directory.
}, onError);
</script>
</body>
</html>
```

# Removing Directories

There are two ways to remove a DirectoryEntry from the filesystem, remove() and removeRecursively().

The first method has the same semantics as FileEntry.remove(), taking an optional callback on successful deletion. However, if you attempt to delete a directory that is not empty, the API throws an error. Making the analogy to UNIX, the same error occurs when calling rmdir on a nonempty folder:

```
dirEntry.remove(function() {
  console.log('Directory removed.');
}, onError);
```

## Recursively Removing a Directory

There are certain situations when you just want to nuke an entire folder, regardless of what it contains. This is where DirectoryEntry.removeRecursively() comes in handy. If you have a pesky directory that contains data, removeRecursively() recursively deletes the directory and all of its contents. If an error occurs while this method is in progress, some of the directory's contents might not be deleted. Be sure to catch that case in your error callback and retry the deletion.

The following snippet fetches the directory *music* and recursively removes it and all the entries it contains:

```
window.requestFileSystem(TEMPORARY, 1024*1024 /*1MB*/, function(fs) {
  fs.root.getDirectory('/misc/music', {}, function(dirEntry) {

    dirEntry.removeRecursively(function() {
      console.log('Directory removed.');
    }, onError);

  }, onError);
}, onError);
```

Both of the remove methods throw an error if you try to remove the root directory in the filesystem (e.g., `fs.root`).

# CHAPTER 6

# Copying, Renaming, and Moving Entries

`FileEntry` and `DirectoryEntry` share common API calls for common tasks such as copying, renaming, and moving an entry. This chapter covers these operations in a generic way, but the concepts can be applied to either entry type.

## Copying a File or Directory

Copying a file or folder to a different location on the filesystem is possible with `copyTo()`. By design, copying a folder is recursive, while files are simply duplicated:

```
entry.copyTo(parentDirEntry, opt_newName, opt_successCallback, opt_errorCallback);
```

The first parameter is a `DirectoryEntry`, the parent folder to move the entry into. The second argument is an optional new name to give the copied entry. The third and fourth parameters are our usual suspects, a success and error callback.

> Attempting to copy an entry in an illegal way can result in an error. Two common errors are trying to copy an entry inside itself and trying to copy an entry in the same folder without specifying a new name.

As an example usage, the following snippet copies the file *me.png* from one directory to another.

*Example 6-1. Copying a file to a different folder*

```
/**
 * Copies a file to a different folder.
 *
 * @param {DirectoryEntry} cwd The current working directory.
 * @param {string} srcFile A relative path from the cwd to a file.
 * @param {string} dest A relative path of the destination directory.
 */
function copyFile(cwd, srcFile, dest) {
```

```
        cwd.getFile(srcFile, {}, function(fileEntry) {

          cwd.getDirectory(dest, {}, function(dirEntry) {
            fileEntry.copyTo(dirEntry);
          }, onError);

        }, onError);
}

window.requestFileSystem(TEMPORARY, 1024*1024 /*1MB*/, function(fs) {
  copyFile(fs.root, '/folder1/me.png', 'folder2/mypics/');
}, onError);
```

Instead, let's say you wanted to duplicate the file in its current location. One way to do that would be to fetch the source file, lookup its parent directory, and pass in a new name to copyTo().

*Example 6-2. Duplicating a file in its current folder*

```
/**
 * Duplicates a file in it's current folder.
 *
 * @param {DirectoryEntry} cwd The current working directory.
 * @param {string} src Relative path from the cwd to a file.
 * @param {string} newName A name for the duplicated file.
 */
function duplicate(cwd, src, newName) {
  cwd.getFile(src, {}, function(fileEntry) {
    fileEntry.getParent(function(destDir) {
      fileEntry.copyTo(destDir, newName, function(copy) {
        console.log(fileEntry.name + ' duplicated as ' + copy.name);
      }, onError);
    }, onError);
  }, onError);
}

window.requestFileSystem(TEMPORARY, 1024*1024 /*1MB*/, function(fs) {
  duplicate(fs.root, 'pics/me.png', 'you.png');
}, onError);
```

Remember, folders are always copied recursively. There is no way to prevent that default behavior.

Taking convenience to the max, we can create a generic utility method that handles both file and directory copies. Said convenience doesn't come for free, however. The solution requires a nested getFile()/getDirectory() combination and an asynchronous nightmare of trial and error.

*Example 6-3. Copy utility that handles file and folders*

```
/**
 * Copies a file or directory.
 *
 * @param {DirectoryEntry} cwd The current working directory.
```

```
 * @param {string} src Relative path to the file/directory to copy.
 * @param {string} dest Relative path to the destination directory.
 * @param {string=} opt_newName An optional name for the copied entry.
 */
function copy(cwd, src, dest, opt_newName) {

  var myCopyTo = function(srcEntry, destEntry, opt_newName) {
    var newName = opt_newName || null;

    srcEntry.copyTo(destEntry, newName, function(copy) {
      console.log(srcEntry.fullPath + ' copied to ' + copy.fullPath);
    }, onError);
  };

  cwd.getDirectory(dest, {}, function(destDir) {

    // First, try src as a file.
    cwd.getFile(src, {}, function(srcFileEntry) {
      myCopyTo(srcFileEntry, destDir, opt_newName);
    }, function(e) {
      if (e.code == FileError.TYPE_MISMATCH_ERR) { // src is actually a dir.
        cwd.getDirectory(src, {}, function(srcDirEntry) {
          myCopyTo(srcDirEntry, destDir, opt_newName);
        }, onError);
      } else {
        onError(e); // Other type of error. Pass through e to our error handler.
      }
    });

  }, onError);
}

window.requestFileSystem(TEMPORARY, 1024*1024 /*1MB*/, function(fs) {
  // '/pics/me.png' copied to '/pics/memories/me.png'
  copy(fs.root, '/pics/me.png', 'pics/memories/');
}, onError);
```

## Moving a File or Directory

After mastering copyTo(), moving an entry will look like a rerun. The method for moving a file or folder is, you guessed it, moveTo():

```
entry.moveTo(parentDir, opt_newName, opt_successCallback, opt_errorCallback);
```

The signature for moveTo() is the same as copyTo(). The first parameter is a directory to move the entry to, the second is an optional new name, and the last two are callbacks. If a new name isn't provided, the file or directory's original name is preserved.

The following example moves *me.png* (located in the root directory) to a folder named *newfolder*.

*Example 6-4. Moving a file to a different directory*

```
/**
 * Moves a file to a different directory.
 *
 * @param {FileSystem} fs The filesystem.
 * @param {string} srcPath Path to a file, relative to the root folder.
 * @param {string} destPath A directory path, relative to the root,
 *      to move the file into.
 */
function move(fs, srcPath, destPath) {
  fs.root.getFile(srcPath, {}, function(fileEntry) {

    fs.root.getDirectory(destPath, {}, function(dirEntry) {
      fileEntry.moveTo(dirEntry);
    }, onError);

  }, onError);
}

window.requestFileSystem(TEMPORARY, 1024*1024 /*1MB*/, function(fs) {
  move(fs, '/me.png', 'newfolder/');
}, onError);
```

Notice that there are no callbacks passed to the move() helper. While this is perfectly acceptable, a real application would want to deal with any errors. Otherwise, erroneous operations fail silently.

# Renaming a File or Directory

When moving a file or directory, you have the option to rename. moveTo() accepts an optional new name as its second parameter. However, sometimes you may want to rename an entry, leaving it in its current directory. moveTo() is somewhat deceptive in that way. The same method is used for both moving and renaming.

Here is an example of renaming a directory.

*Example 6-5. Renaming a directory*

```
**
 * Moves a file to a different directory.
 *
 * @param {DirectoryEntry} cwd The current working directory.
 * @param {string} srcDir Path to a directory, relative to the cwd.
 * @param {function(DirectoryEntry)=} opt_successCallback An optional
 *      success callback passed the updated directory.
 */
function rename(cwd, srcDir, newName, opt_successCallback) {
  cwd.getDirectory(srcDir, {}, function(dirEntry) {
    fileEntry.moveTo(cwd, newName, opt_successCallback);
  }, onError);
}
```

```
window.requestFileSystem(TEMPORARY, 1024*1024 /*1MB*/, function(fs) {
  rename(fs.root, '/media/photos', 'pics', function(entry) {
    console.log(entry.name + ' was moved successfully');
  ));
}, onError);
```

# CHAPTER 7

# Using Files

Chapter 4 focused on common operations for working with files such as reading, writing, and removing files. It did not discuss in detail the ways in which an application can utilize a file residing in its filesystem. However, in most scenarios, you do not need to read the contents of a file in order to use it.

## Filesystem URLs

Perhaps the easiest way to use a file is to reference it by URL. The HTML5 Filesystem API exposes a new type of URL scheme, `filesystem:`. The structure of a filesystem URL is as follows:

```
filesystem:<ORIGIN>/<STORAGE_TYPE>/<FILENAME>
```

The format is the scheme, `filesystem:`, followed by the application's origin, the storage type the filesystem was requested with, and finally, the full path of the file or folder as it resides on the filesystem. For example, if your application lived at *http://www.example .com/myapp* and used `PERSISTENT` storage, the filesystem URL to the root folder would be: *filesystem:http://www.example/temporary/*.

So why are filesystem URLs handy? They're useful because they can be used anywhere a normal URL can be used. For example, you could cache a *.js* file and later use that file's URL to fill a `script.src` on demand. You could do the same with a *.html* file, but instead populate an `iframe.src`. Lastly, you could display an image by setting its `src` to a filesystem URL.

Currently in Chrome, filesystem URLs are guessable—one can be constructed manually by knowing the proper format. This might not always be the case and other browser implementations might choose a different format as the specification becomes standardized. For these reasons, the API contains methods for obtaining and resolving these URLs.

To obtain a filesystem URL for a `FileEntry` or `DirectoryEntry`, call to its `toURL()` method:

```
var img = document.createElement('img');
img.src = fileEntry.toURL();
// e.g. 'filesystem:http://www.example/temporary/path/to/file.png'
document.body.appendChild(img);
```

 Chrome currently does not have a dedicated UI for browsing the files stored in a filesystem. Even the Developer Tools (*http://code.google.com/ chrome/devtools/docs/overview.html*) do not expose this data in the Resources tab. To view your filesystem for debugging purposes, open a browser tab to the root folder:

`fs.root.toURL()` (e.g., *filesystem:http://www.example/temporary/*)

Given one of these URLs, the global method `resolveLocalFileSystemURL()` will get you back to `FileEntry` or `DirectoryEntry` object. It takes a filesystem URL, success callback, and error callback:

```
const URL = 'filesystem:http://www.example/temporary/path/to/file.png';

window.resolveLocalFileSystemURL(URL, function(entry) {
  // entry.isFile === true
}, onError);
```

 This method is currently prefixed as `window.webkitResolveLocalFile SystemURL()`.

Now that we have a new way of referencing files and folders, let's revisit Example 6-3 from Chapter 6. Before we used `entry.getFile()` and `entry.getDirectory()` to lookup the file and destination folder entries. This time we'll use `resolveLocalFileSystemURL()`.

*Example 7-1. Copy utility from Example 6-3, but using resolveLocalFileSystemURL()*

```
/**
 * Copies a file or directory.
 *
 * @param {DirectoryEntry} cwd The current working directory.
 * @param {string} src Relative path to the file/directory to copy.
 * @param {string} dest Relative path to the destination directory.
 * @param {string=} opt_newName An optional name for the copied entry.
 */
function copy(cwd, src, dest, opt_newName) {
  window.resolveLocalFileSystemURL = window.resolveLocalFileSystemURL ||
                                     window.webkitResolveLocalFileSystemURL;

  // e.g. "filesystem:http://example.com/temporary/"
  var baseFsUrl = cwd.filesystem.root.toURL();
```

```
  window.resolveLocalFileSystemURL(baseFsUrl + dest, function(destDir) {
    if (!destDir.isDirectory) {
      throw 'Oops! ' + destDir.name + ' is not a directory!';
    }
    window.resolveLocalFileSystemURL(baseFsUrl + src, function(entry) {
      entry.copyTo(destDir, opt_newName || null, function(copy) {
        console.log(entry.fullPath + ' copied to ' + copy.fullPath);
      }, onError);
    }, onError);
  }, onError);
}

window.requestFileSystem(TEMPORARY, 1024*1024 /*1MB*/, function(fs) {
  // '/pics/me.png' copied to '/pics/memories/me.png'
  copy(fs.root, '/pics/me.png', 'pics/memories/');

  // '/pics/me.png' copied to '/pics/memories/you.png'
  // copy(fs.root, '/pics/me.png', 'pics/memories/', 'you.png');

  // '/pics/' copied to '/pics2/'
  // copy(fs.root, '/pics/', '/', 'pics2');
}, onError);
```

As you can tell, the code cleans up nicely. Most importantly, we're no longer abusing error callbacks by trying to recover from calling the wrong get method on src.

## Summary

Pros:

- Persistent URL to a resource in the filesystem.
- Can be used as a src or href attribute.
- Can construct manually.

Cons:

- File must be stored in the filesystem.

# Blob URLs

Another way to use a File is to create a blob URL, also referred to as an object URL. This approach lets you create a unique handle to a File or Blob object. The structure of a blob URL is as follow:

    blob:<ORIGIN>/<UNIQUE_RANDOM_STR>

The format is the scheme, blob:, followed by the application's origin, and a random string generated by the browser. Since these URLs are generated by the browser, it is not possible to manually construct a blob URL. For example, if your application lived at *http://www.example.com/myapp* a blob URL generated for a particular File might look like *blob:http://www.example/d8c2c85e-ab1b*. Generating a second might look to-tally different: *blob:http://www.example/zbebf235e-s1b*.

Create a blob URL from a file-like object using `window.URL.createObjectURL()`:

```
var blobUrl = window.URL.createObjectURL(file);
```

In WebKit and Chrome, this method is currently prefixed:

`window.webkitURL.createObjectURL()`

It's important to remember that the browser creates a memory reference to the file/blob on every call to `window.URL.createObjectURL()`. The result is a unique string that lasts for the lifetime of the application (e.g., until the document is unloaded). However, if an application uses many blob URLs dynamically, it's a good idea to release any refer-ences that are no longer needed. You can explicitly revoke a blob URL by calling `window.URL.revokeObjectURL()`:

```
window.URL.revokeObjectURL(blobUrl);
```

This method is currently prefixed as `window.webkitURL.revokeObjec tURL()`in Webkit and Chrome.

Chrome has a nice about page for viewing outstanding blob URLs, which you can access at: *chrome://blob-internals/*.

The following example fetches all entries in the root directory, filters out the image files, and uses `window.URL.createObjectURL()` to render the images.

*Example 7-2. Using Blob URLs to view images in the filesystem*

```
<!DOCTYPE html>
<html>
<head>
  <meta charset="utf-8">
  <title>Using Blob URLs to view images in the filesystem.</title>
</head>
<body>
<script>
// Take care of vendor prefixes.
window.requestFileSystem = window.requestFileSystem ||
                           window.webkiRequestFileSystem;
window.URL = window.URL || window.webkitURL;

function toArray(list) {
  return Array.prototype.slice.call(list || [], 0);
```

```
}
function renderImages(fs) {

  var dirReader = fs.root.createReader(); // Create reader for root directory.
  var entries = [];

  // Call the reader.readEntries() until no more results are returned.
  var readEntries = function() {
    dirReader.readEntries(function(results) {

      if (!results.length) { // We're done. No more results.

        entries.forEach(function(entry, i) {
          if (entry.isFile) {
            entry.file(function(file) {

              if (file.type.match(/image.*/)) { // We only care about images.

                var img = document.createElement('img');
                img.onload = function(e) {
                  window.URL.revokeObjectURL(this.src); // Clean up.
                };
                img.src = window.URL.createObjectURL(file);

                document.body.append(img);
              }

            }, onError);
          }
        });

      } else {
        // Add in these results to the current list.
        entries = entries.concat(toArray(results));
        readEntries();
      }
    }, onError);
  };

  readEntries(); // Start reading the directory.
}

window.requestFileSystem(TEMPORARY, 1024*1024 /*1MB*/, renderImages, onError);
</script>
</body>
</html>
```

You're not limited to passing a File to window.URL.createObjectURL(). It also accepts Blob data. Using the BlobBuilder API, one can programmatically create a "file", then reference it via a URL. For example, this snippet creates a stylesheet programmatically and adds it to the page:

```
window.URL = window.URL || window.webkitURL;
window.BlobBuilder = window.BlobBuilder || window.WebKitBlobBuilder ||
```

```
                    window.MozBlobBuilder;

    var bb = new BlobBuilder();
    bb.append('body { background-color: red; }');

    var link = document.createElement('link');
    link.rel = 'stylesheet';
    link.href = window.URL.createObjectURL(bb.getBlob('text/css'));

    document.head.appendChild(link);
```

One clever use of this trick is to create an "inline" Web Worker. Normally workers are initialized by an external script (e.g., `var worker = new Worker('task.js')`). The file has to live somewhere on the server and requires a network request to fetch. Instead, let's dynamically create the file from code living on the same HTML page as the main app logic—a single page multithreaded app!

*Example 7-3. Inline Web Worker thanks to blob URLs*

```
<!DOCTYPE html>
<html>
<head>
  <meta charset="utf-8" />
  <title>Inline Web Worker</title>
</head>
<body>
  <script id="worker1" type="javascript/worker">
    // This script won't be parsed by the JS engine because its
    // type is not text/javascript.
    self.onmessage = function(e) {
      self.postMessage('Hi from worker');
    };
    // Rest of your worker code goes here.
  </script>
  <script>
    // Take care of prefixes.
    window.URL = window.URL || window.webkitURL;
    window.BlobBuilder = window.BlobBuilder || window.WebKitBlobBuilder ||
                         window.MozBlobBuilder;

    var bb = new BlobBuilder();
    bb.append(document.querySelector('[type="javascript/worker"]').textContent);

    var worker = new Worker(window.URL.createObjectURL(bb.getBlob()));

    worker.onmessage = function(e) {
      console.log('Received: ' + e.data);
    }

    worker.postMessage(); // Start the worker.
  </script>
</body>
</html>
```

When using this trick, always remember to change the type attribute of the inline `<script>`, otherwise the browser will stop the parser and interpret the code as normal JavaScript.

## Summary

Pros:

- Temporary (and unique) URL handle to the content.
- Can be used as a `src` or `href` attribute.

Cons:

- Cannot construct manually.
- Doesn't come for free. Use `window.URL.revokeObjectURL()` to release memory references.

# Data URLs

My final technique for using a file is to encode its content in a data URL. Many developers are familiar with data URLs. Out of the three URL types covered in this chapter, they are by far the most supported. All the major browsers support data URLs, including IE8 and up. If you're not familiar with a data URL, the structure is as follows:

```
data:<mimetype>[;base64],<data>
```

The format is the scheme, `data:`, followed by a mimetype string such as "image/jpeg", ";base64" if the data is base64 encoded, and the data content.

Data URLs are a bit different than the other URL types discussed earlier in this chapter. With filesystem URLs, content is referenced by a URL the browser understands and for blob URLs, a handle to the content is created with `window.URL.createObjectURL()`. The key difference in a data URL is that the content itself is encoded in the URL. Both filesystem and blob URLs reference content. Data URLs *are* the content. They are also browser agnostic. A nice property that comes from these facts is that data URLs can be shared. For example, I can send friends a data URL and they can open that content in the browser. The same isn't true with the other URLs.

Many people use data URLs as background images in stylesheets or for small sprite images because it saves an HTTP request. Data URLs can also be used directly in `src` and `href` attributes:

```
var link = document.createElement('link');
link.rel = 'stylesheet';
link.href = 'data:text/css,body { background: red; }');

document.head.appendChild(link);
```

If you're working with a binary string (e.g., the result of a `FileR eader.readAsBinaryString()`), use the browser's native `window.btoa()` to base64 encode that content for a data URL:

```
var audio = document.createElement('audio');
audio.src = 'data:audio/ogg;base64,' + window.btoa(binaryStr);

document.body.appendChild(audio);
```

Lastly, data URLs also show up in the `FileReader` API. To read a file as data URL, call `readAsDataURL()`.

*Example 7-4. Reading a file as a data URL*

```
function readAsDataURL(fileEntry) {

  if (!fileEntry.isFile) {
    alert('Not a file!');
  }

  fileEntry.file(function(file) {

    var reader = new FileReader();

    reader.onerror - function(e) {
      console.log('Oops!', e);
    };

    reader.onload = function(e) {
      var img = document.createElement('img');
      img.title = file.name;
      img.alt = file.name;
      img.src = e.target.result;

      document.body.appendChild(img);
    };

    reader.readAsDataURL(file); // Read in the file as a data URL.

  }, onError);
}

window.resolveLocalFileSystemURL(
    'filesystem:http://www.example/temporary/path/to/image.png',
    readAsDataURL, onError);
```

## Summary

Pros:

- Persistent. URL contains the content.
- Can be used as a `src` or `href` attribute.

- Can construct manually.
- Saves 1 less HTTP request.

Cons:

- Not separately cached, so data is downloaded every time.
- Base64 encoding binary data adds a 33% overhead to the file size. Some browser impose restrictions to the size of data URLs.
- Have to read an entire file into memory to create a data URL from it.

 If you ever need a quick code editor during a presentation, use a data URL as your IDE! Open this in a new tab:

```
data:text/html,<pre contenteditable
    style='font:30pt;height:70%;border:1px solid #ccc;'></pre>
```

# CHAPTER 8

# The Synchronous API

## Introduction

The HTML5 Filesystem API includes a synchronous version that, for the most part, is exactly the same as its asynchronous cousin. The methods, properties, features, and functionality will be familiar. The major deviations are:

- The synchronous API can only be used within a Web Worker context. The asynchronous API can be used in and out of a worker.
- Callbacks are out. API methods now return values.
- The global methods on the `window` object (`requestFileSystem()` and `resolveLocal FileSystemURL()`) are renamed as `requestFileSystemSync()` and `resolveLocalFile SystemSyncURL()` and members of the worker's global scope.

The two APIs are the same, save these few exceptions. Because there is not much new to cover, this chapter won't cover the synchronous API in great detail. I'll only highlight the exceptions to the asynchronous API and provide a few examples to make things clear.

## Opening a Filesystem

A web application obtains access to the synchronous filesystem by requesting a `Local FileSystemSync` object from within a web worker. The `requestFileSystemSync()` is exposed to the worker's global scope:

```
var fs = requestFileSystemSync(TEMPORARY, 1024*1024 /*1MB*/);
```

 This method is currently vendor prefixed as `webkitRequestFileSystem Sync`.

The reader should note two things about this call: the new return value and the absence of success and error callbacks.

## Working with Files and Directories

The synchronous filesystem has a `getFile()` and `getDirectory()` which return a `FileEntrySync` and `DirectoryEntrySync`, respectively.

For example, the following code creates an empty file called "log.txt" in the root directory.

*Example 8-1. Creating a file*

```
var fileEntry = fs.root.getFile('log.txt', {create: true});
```

The following creates a new directory in the root folder.

*Example 8-2. Creating a directory*

```
var dirEntry = fs.root.getDirectory('mydir', {create: true});
```

## Handling Errors

The lack of error callbacks in the synchronous world makes dealing with problems tricky. Add to that the complexity of debugging in a web worker, and you'll be pulling out your hair in no time. One thing that you can do to make life easier is wrap all of the relevant worker code in a try/catch. If any errors occur, forward it to the main app using `postMessage()`.

*Example 8-3. Error handling in a worker*

```
function onError(e) {
  postMessage('ERROR: ' + e.toString());
}

try {
  // Error thrown if "log.txt" already exists.
  var fileEntry = fs.root.getFile('log.txt', {create: true, exclusive: true});
} catch (e) {
  onError(e);
}
```

## Examples

This section contains two full examples that you may find useful. Feel free to incorporate them into your own projects.

## Fetching All Entries in the Filesystem

Some may argue that the synchronous API is much cleaner. Fewer callbacks are nice and they certainly make things more readable. The real disadvantage of the synchronous filesystem is due to the limitations of web workers.

For security reasons, data between an app and a web worker thread is never shared. It is copied to and from the worker using the postMessage() API. As such, only primitive types (Array, Number, Boolean, ...) can be passed using postMessage(). Unfortunately, this means that FileEntrySync and DirectoryEntrySync are not included in the list. They are not serializable types.

One option for getting entries back to the main app is to return a filesystem: URL instead of the entry itself. Since these URLs are just strings, it is very easy for the main app to use a filesystem: URL as it sees fit.

*Example 8-4. Fetching all entries and passing them back to the main app (worker.js)*

```
self.requestFileSystemSync =  self.webkitRequestFileSystemSync ||
                              self.requestFileSystemSync;

var paths = [];

function getAllEntries(dirReader) {

  var entries = dirReader.readEntries();

  for (var i = 0, entry; entry = entries[i]; ++i) {
    paths.push(entry.toURL());

    // If this is a directory, we have more traversing to do.
    if (entry.isDirectory) {
      getAllEntries(entry.createReader());
    }
  }
}

function onError(e) {
  postMessage('ERROR: ' + e.toString());
}

self.onmessage = function(e) {
  var data = e.data;

  // Ignore everything else accept the 'list' command.
  if (!data.cmd || data.cmd != 'list') {
    return;
  }

  try {
    var fs = requestFileSystemSync(TEMPORARY, 1024*1024 /*1MB*/);

    getAllEntries(fs.root.createReader());
```

```
      self.postMessage({entries: paths});

  } catch (e) {
    onError(e);
  }
};
```

Main app:

```
<!DOCTYPE html>
<html>
<head>
<meta charset="utf-8" />
<meta http-equiv="X-UA-Compatible" content="chrome=1">
<title>Listing filesystem entries using the synchronous API</title>
</head>
<body>
<script>
  var worker = new Worker('worker.js');
  worker.onmessage = function(e) {
    console.log(e.data.entries);
  }
  worker.postMessage({'cmd': 'list'});
</script>
</body>
</html>
```

## Downloading Files Using XHR2

A common use case for using web workers is to download a bunch of files using XHR2, and write those files to the HTML5 filesystem. A perfect task for a worker thread!

The following example only fetches and writes one file, but you can image expanding it to download a set of files.

*Example 8-5. Downloading files using XHR2 (downloader.js)*

```
self.requestFileSystemSync =  self.webkitRequestFileSystemSync ||
                              self.requestFileSystemSync;
self.BlobBuilder = self.WebKitBlobBuilder || self.MozBlobBuilder ||
                   self.BlobBuilder;

function makeRequest(url) {
  try {
    var xhr = new XMLHttpRequest();
    xhr.open('GET', url, false); // Synchronous
    xhr.responseType = 'arraybuffer';
    xhr.send();
    return xhr.response;
  } catch(e) {
    return "XHR Error " + e.toString();
  }
}
```

```
function onError(e) {
  postMessage('ERROR: ' + e.toString());
}

onmessage = function(e) {
  var data = e.data;

  // Make sure we have the right parameters.
  if (!data.fileName || !data.url || !data.type) {
    return;
  }

  try {
    var fs = requestFileSystemSync(TEMPORARY, 1024*1024 /*1MB*/);

    postMessage('Got file system.');

    var fileEntry = fs.root.getFile(data.fileName, {create: true});

    postMessage('Got file handle.');

    var writer = fileEntry.createWriter();
    writer.onerror = onError;
    writer.onwrite = function(e) {
      postMessage('Write complete!');
      postMessage(fileEntry.toURL());
    };

    var bb = new BlobBuilder();
    bb.append(makeRequest(data.url)); // Append the arrayBuffer XHR response.

    postMessage('Begin writing');

    writer.write(bb.getBlob(data.type))

  } catch (e) {
    onError(e);
  }
};
```

Main app:

```
<!DOCTYPE html>
<html>
<head>
<meta charset="utf-8" />
<meta http-equiv="X-UA-Compatible" content="chrome=1">
<title>Download files using a XHR2, a worker, and saving to filesystem</title>
</head>
<body>
<script>
  var worker = new Worker('downloader.js');
  worker.onmessage = function(e) {
    console.log(e.data);
  }
  worker.postMessage(
```

```
        {fileName: 'GoogleLogo', url: 'google_logo.png', type: 'image/png'});
</script>
</body>
</html>
```

## About the Author

**Eric Bidelman** is a Senior Developer Programs Engineer on the Google Chrome team, and one of the core contributors to html5rocks.com. His mission is to spread HTML5 goodness by educating developers worldwide. Eric previously worked on Google Docs, Sites, Health, and OAuth APIs. Prior to Google, Eric worked as a software engineer at the University of Michigan where he designed rich web applications and APIs for the university's 19 libraries. Eric holds a B.S.E in Computer Engineering and a B.S.E in Electrical Engineering from the University of Michigan, Ann Arbor. He can be found on Twitter at *@ebidel*.

## Colophon

The animal on the cover of *Using the HTML5 Filesystem API* is a Russian greyhound.

The cover image is from J. G. Wood's *Animate Creation*. The cover font is Adobe ITC Garamond. The text font is Linotype Birka; the heading font is Adobe Myriad Condensed; and the code font is LucasFont's TheSansMonoCondensed.

# Get even more for your money.

**Join the O'Reilly Community, and register the O'Reilly books you own. It's free, and you'll get:**

- $4.99 ebook upgrade offer
- 40% upgrade offer on O'Reilly print books
- Membership discounts on books and events
- Free lifetime updates to ebooks and videos
- Multiple ebook formats, DRM FREE
- Participation in the O'Reilly community
- Newsletters
- Account management
- 100% Satisfaction Guarantee

**Signing up is easy:**

1. Go to: oreilly.com/go/register
2. Create an O'Reilly login.
3. Provide your address.
4. Register your books.

Note: English-language books only

**To order books online:**
oreilly.com/store

**For questions about products or an order:**
orders@oreilly.com

**To sign up to get topic-specific email announcements and/or news about upcoming books, conferences, special offers, and new technologies:**
elists@oreilly.com

**For technical questions about book content:**
booktech@oreilly.com

**To submit new book proposals to our editors:**
proposals@oreilly.com

**O'Reilly books are available in multiple DRM-free ebook formats. For more information:**
oreilly.com/ebooks

Spreading the knowledge of innovators          oreilly.com

# The information you need, when and where you need it.

## With Safari Books Online, you can:

### Access the contents of thousands of technology and business books

- Quickly search over 7000 books and certification guides
- Download whole books or chapters in PDF format, at no extra cost, to print or read on the go
- Copy and paste code
- Save up to 35% on O'Reilly print books
- **New!** Access mobile-friendly books directly from cell phones and mobile devices

### Stay up-to-date on emerging topics before the books are published

- Get on-demand access to evolving manuscripts.
- Interact directly with authors of upcoming books

### Explore thousands of hours of video on technology and design topics

- Learn from expert video tutorials
- Watch and replay recorded conference sessions

Lightning Source UK Ltd.
Milton Keynes UK
UKHW031947111122
412045UK00011B/468